Two cards from the Hofämterspiel pack issued in Austria about 1460. The pack consists of 48 hand-coloured wood engravings and has four suits of shields relating to four states of the period: Germany, France, Bohemia and Hungary. The figures, which appear on all cards, depict courtly personages and employees of the royal households. The two cards illustrated are a Two (of Germany) showing a letter-carrier, and a Three (of Bohemia) showing a herald. The cards are preserved in the Kunsthistorisches Museum in Vienna.

PLAYING-CARDS AND TAROTS

George Beal

Shire Publications Ltd

CONTENTS

Set in 9 point Times roman and printed in Great Britain by C. I. Thomas & Sons (Haverfordwest) Ltd, Press Buildings, Merlins Bridge, Haverfordwest, Dyfed.

British Library Cataloguing in Publication Data available.

Cover: *(Top row, from left to right) A Chinese domino-type playing-card; a Russian Queen of Hearts (non-standard pack); an Indian ganjifa court card. (Bottom row) The Three of Coins from a Japanese pack; a nineteenth-century German non-standard King of Leaves; the Hanging Man trump from a Marseilles Tarot pack.*

An illustration taken from the book 'Das Guldin Spil', published in 1472, and showing card-players using German-suited playing-cards.

An early illustration showing playing-card manufacture, in which stencils are being used to add colour and suitmarks.

THE ORIGIN OF PLAYING-CARDS

For centuries people have speculated on the origin of playing-cards. Some theories have it that they came from the East: from China perhaps, or India. So many interesting things originated in China that it is not surprising that it should be named as the home of playing-cards — which have been said to exist in the T'ang Dynasty (AD 618 to 907). A Chinese encyclopaedia of 1678, however, gives 1120 as the precise date of their invention, but there is no other evidence to substantiate this. Moreover there is no evidence that Chinese cards were the originals of the European versions.

The earliest references to playing-cards in India go back no further than the sixteenth century. The late Dr Rudolf von Leyden put forward the theory that they could have followed a trade route from India across Asia to the Middle East. However, neither Indian nor Chinese cards are like western patterns, although it is possible to show some links in their design.

One claim is that playing-cards were brought to Europe by gypsies, while another suggests that crusaders brought them back from the Holy Land. Neither idea is likely to be correct. The last crusade ended in 1291, and our first knowledge of playing-cards in Europe is about a hundred years after this. Gypsies first appeared in Europe in 1398, by which time playing-cards were well known. However, these theories have one thing in common — they suggest a Middle Eastern origin.

There are few early European references, but one of the earliest is a docu-

A German engraving dated 1500 showing the Grand Duke and Duchess of Bavaria playing cards.

Three cards from the Mameluke pack showing (left to right): a court card depicting the Second Viceroy from the Cups suit; the Two of Cups; the Six of Polo-sticks.

ment published in Basel, Switzerland, in 1377. The author, John of Rheinfelden, describes playing-cards in considerable detail and states that they reached Switzerland in the year in which he wrote. He did not know their origin, but another writer, Giovanni de Covelluzzo, writing in the fifteenth century, suggests that a card-game called *Naib* was brought to Viterbo in 1379 from 'Seracinia' (presumably the country of the Saracens). So here is evidence that playing-cards were known in Italy close to the date mentioned by John of Rheinfelden. The word *na'ib* is Arabic and means 'deputy'. Malespini, in his *History of Florence* published in 1728, quotes a document of 1393 by Giovanni Morelli who refers to *Naibi* as a kind of game. The word *naipes* is still used in Spain, meaning simply 'playing-cards'. The Spaniards had close connections with Islamic countries, which accords with Covelluzzo's suggestion that playing-cards came from the Saracens, an Islamic people.

From all this it seems a reasonable assumption that western cards originated from some Arabic source. Yet Islam is strict about all forms of gambling; could there have been true Islamic playing-cards? It seemed doubtful until such a pack was found in 1939 in the Topkapi Sarayi Museum in Istanbul. A few cards are missing, but it had obviously consisted of 52 cards. Its Islamic connection is certain, so here is the link. The pack, with designs closely resembling those used in Italy, dates from the Mameluke dynasty in Egypt (1254-1517), and its manufacture has been expertly dated to the fifteenth century. While this is later than the first known cards in Europe, a fragment of a card from another Mame-luke pack, and which is undoubtedly of the twelfth century, exists in the same museum.

The Mameluke pack and any standard Italian pack show remarkable resemblances. Both contain 52 cards divided into four suits, identified as Cups, Coins, Swords and Polo-sticks. In each suit the Mameluke pack has three court cards: *malik* (king), *na'ib malik* (deputy king, governor or viceroy), and *na'ib thani* (deputy governor), as well as ten numerical cards. True to Islamic art, the Mameluke pack uses arabesque designs and does not depict actual persons.

Thus it has been established that Islamic playing-cards arrived in Europe by way of Italy from the Middle East, but was that their true origin? Dr von Leyden supposes that playing-cards came from India and may be derived from the eastern game of four-sided chess. While this offers an explanation of the courts and numerical cards, no evidence has been found to substantiate this suggestion.

PLAYING-CARDS IN ITALY, SPAIN AND PORTUGAL

As we have seen, the first playing-cards known in Europe were found in Italy. The Mameluke cards are large, measuring 252 by 95 mm (10 by 3¾ inches), although similar in format to Italian cards. However the fragment found in Istanbul would have produced a card measuring 116 by 78 mm (4½ by 3 inches), very similar to the size still used in Italy.

John of Rheinfelden does not describe the suitmarks of the playing-cards he mentions, but one can deduce that they must have been like those adopted later in Germany. In Italy the suitmarks closely followed the Islamic originals but became more identifiable to European eyes. Italian suitmarks are Swords, *Spade;* Cups, *Coppe;* Coins, *Danari* or *Denari;* and Batons, *Bastoni.* The court cards are King, Knight and Jack, thus following the all-male tradition set by Islamic cards. Italian suitmarks fall into two main groups: the traditional patterns similar to the earliest designs — still being used in north-west Italy, and a rather simpler version appearing in the southern parts of the country. Until 1861 Italy was not one country but several independent states. Thus a number of packs existed with varying but standard regional designs.

Closely linked with the patterns of southern Italy are those of Spain and Portugal. Again the suitmarks are Swords, Cups, Coins and Batons; so we find that Spain and the regions of Naples, Sicily, Rome and Sardinia developed similar playing-card designs. The north-western regions of Italy, Venice and Trieste remained closer to the Islamic original.

The commonest pack is that used in the Venetian region, known as *Venete, Trevi-*

Above: *Three cards from a North Italian pack dating from the fifteenth century, showing the Nine of Swords, the Five of Cups and the Six of Coins.*

Left: *The Italian and Spanish suits of Coins, Cups, Swords and Batons.*

giane or *Trevisane telate*. The Venetian pattern contains forty cards, occasionally more, with each of the four suits having ten or more cards. A distinguishing feature is the use on the aces of mottoes such as *Non val saper a chi ha fortuna contra* in the Coins suit. This is not standard Italian but Venetian dialect and means 'It is not worth knowing someone whose luck is always out'. Other packs in north-western Italy are found in Trieste, Trento, Bergamo and Brescia, all of them variations of the Venetian pattern.

Since the end of the nineteenth century, most Italian packs have been double-ended, but earlier single-ended cards are found. On these, and the present-day Trentine pattern, the court figures are always seated, unlike French and English patterns.

Southern Italy has four more packs using the suitmarks of Swords, Cups,

Coins and Batons, but here they show Italian/Spanish variations. In all four the suitmarks are clearly shown, lacking the intricate arabesques of the north-west Italian type. Southern packs, together with those of Sardinia and Spain, have standing court figures except for the Knight, who is mounted.

An interesting development of the Italian/Spanish patterns occurred in Portugal. Here the traditional Italian style seems to have influenced the design, two of the suits appearing as crossed Swords and Clubs. Instead of King, Knight and Jack, the court cards were King, Queen and Knight, and the aces bore dragons. These packs seem to date back to the sixteenth century. Today Portugal uses a modern pack based on the Paris pattern and using French suitmarks.

Portuguese adventurers carried their cards with them, and even today

Japanese packs contain modified versions of Cups, Swords, Coins, Batons and dragon-aces.

Spain has retained the old suitmarks, but in Italy the north-east areas changed to the French marks of Hearts, Clubs, Diamonds and Spades following the Napoleonic invasion. Packs largely followed French design, though those of Florence and Tuscany adopted courts in a more comic-opera style.

Left: *Two cards from a North Italian pack showing the Six of Batons and the Four of Swords.*

The King of Coins, the Knight of Cups and the Jack of Swords from the modern South Italian pack.

The King of Cups, the Knight of Coins and the Ace of Coins, from a modern Venetian Italian pack.

Above: *The King of Cups, the Knight of Coins and the Ace of Swords from a Portuguese pack. This pack is no longer issued, but it dates back to the fifteenth century, when Portuguese navigators carried the cards to Japan.*

Below: *Part of a sheet of standard Spanish cards as issued during the seventeenth century. The Ace of Swords bears a decorative belt which in the Portuguese version developed into a dragon.*

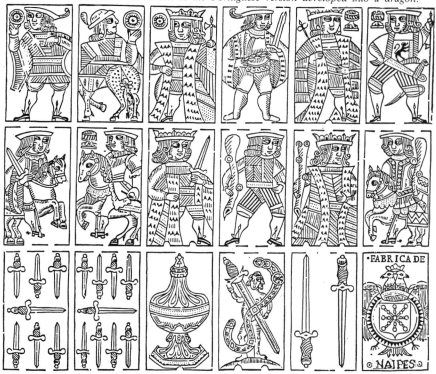

The King of Cups and the Knight of Coins from a standard Spanish pack which is widely used in Spain and her former colonies in Asia, Africa and South and Central America.

THE PLAYING-CARDS OF CENTRAL EUROPE

Once playing-cards were established in Italy they spread rapidly to other parts of Europe. By the second half of the fourteenth century they had become well established in Germany (like Italy, a group of separate states) and neighbouring countries. According to *Das Guldin Spil,* written by a monk named Ingold and published in 1472, playing-cards were taken back to Germany by soldiers returning from Italian wars. Their popularity was immense, and production was aided by the invention of printing around 1450. It is indeed possible that packs of playing-cards were among the earliest items to be printed, preceding even books and pamphlets.

Until that time, playing-cards had to be made by hand. No doubt some were very crude, but few hand-made packs have survived. Printing made all the difference. Wood-blocks were cut and packs printed from these, any colours required being added by hand.

Germany became a world centre for printing playing-cards, and the card-makers became quite inventive in their designs. No doubt the Italian suitmarks arrived and were used in Germany, but soon all sorts of other devices came into use. There were packs with Lions, Monkeys, Peacocks and Parrots; and rival printers would produce packs with Hares, Books, Fishes and Drinking-cups. Eventually the German suitpacks were standardised as Hearts, Hawk-bells, Leaves and Acorns, and they remain so to this day. Local variations took place — for instance in Switzerland the Hearts and Hawk-bells gave way to Flowers and Shields.

As in Italy the court cards were all male: *König, Obermann* and *Untermann,* equivalent to King, Knight and Jack. The King's suitmark appears over his head; the *Obermann* (or *'Ober'*) holds his below his knees.

Central Europe was made up of many small states, and German-suited packs were made and used in what are now East and West Germany, Austria, Hungary, Poland, Czechoslovakia and, with the differences mentioned above, Switzerland. It was inevitable that there were variations in these packs. Even after the unification of both Germany and Austria playing-cards were made that continued regional traditions. Thus today one can

9

The Swiss suits of Shields, Flowers, Acorns and Hawk-bells.

The German suits of Hearts, Leaves, Acorns and Hawk-bells.

Three cards from the Upper Rhine district of Germany, made in 1460, and showing courts with suitmarks of the Bear, the Lion and the Dog.

The King of Hearts, the Ober of Bells and the Deuce of Acorns from the German Ansbacher regional pack formerly used in the Nuremberg area.

The King of Acorns, the Ober of Bells and the Six of Bells from the Salzburger pack, used in Austria. Variants of this design are found in Czechoslovakia and Germany.

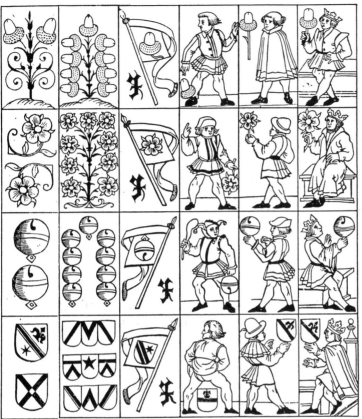

The court cards, the Banners, the Twos and Nines from a Swiss pack made in 1580. The suitmarks are Acorns (Eicheln), Flowers (Rosen), Bells (Schellen) and Shields (Schilten). The Banner card represents a ten, as shown by the stylised letter X.

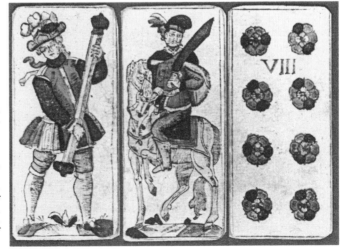

Three cards from a Trappola pack issued in Bohemia at the end of the nineteenth century. This German-style pack uses Italian suitmarks. Shown here are the Jack of Batons, the Knight of Swords and the Eight of Coins. In this example, the Coins are represented by rosettes of flowers.

find local packs in Prussia, Wurttemberg, Nuremberg, Bavaria, Salzburg, Prague, Saxony and Hungary. All these use the standard German suitmarks of Hearts, Hawk-bells, Leaves and Acorns.

Games played with such cards naturally tend to be local. These include a game called 'Tarock', but such packs should not be mistaken for Tarot packs, which are confusingly also known in German as *Tarocke* (see below).

Apart from the standard German-suited cards, Germany and other Central European countries have also adopted packs using French suitmarks. Often these follow the Paris pattern quite closely, but since the nineteenth century it has been fashionable to produce some ornate packs, most of which still use the French suitmark system. One or two French-suited packs have become more or less standard in Germany and Austria. The English pack is also seen.

Another oddity found in central Europe is the Trappola pack. Despite using Italian suitmarks, these cards were not used in Italy but in Germany and Austria-Hungary. They are no longer used, though old packs still exist as curiosities. In style they follow the Germanic tradition, although they are more flamboyant. Usually larger than most cards, the 36-card Trappola pack consists of King, Knight, Jack and numerical cards Seven to Ten plus the Deuce. Packs with double-ended courts are sometimes found, as well as those with aces. The numerical cards are indexed with Roman numerals. Exactly why such cards should have made their way into a basically Teutonic area is not known.

The King of Acorns, the Ober of Bells and the Banner (ten) of Shields, from the standard Swiss pack. The Banner is marked with a sign representing the Roman X or ten.

Two notgeld (German banknotes from the 1922 inflationary period) issued from Altenburg with decorations showing German suitmarks from playing-cards.

Some early cards from France: 'Hector de Trois', a Jack of Diamonds, dated about 1650; 'Rolant', a Jack of Diamonds, dated to the fifteenth century; 'Hogier', a Jack of Spades of the late fifteenth century.

THE FRENCH PACK

Playing-cards arrived in France at about the same time as they reached Germany. At first the Italian suitmarks predominated, but in about 1480 the familiar French ones were devised. Hearts, Clubs, Diamonds and Spades have now become international.

The earliest French cards which still exist are dated 1460, but we know that playing-cards were used in France well before that date since they are mentioned by Laurent Aycardi, a notary from Marseilles, in August 1381. Seventy years later there were numerous French makers printing cards from wood-blocks.

Like the Germans, the French experimented with various suitmarks, but it was the development of simple marks, *Coeurs* (hearts), *Tréfles* (trefoils), *Piques* (pikes) and *Carreaux* (squares or tiles), that enabled the French to become supreme in European card-making. To produce a pack of cards using German or Italian suitmarks the whole pack had to be engraved — a costly operation. Being so simple, the French suitmarks were eminently suited for reproduction by stencil. Thus French packs required only the twelve court cards to be engraved; for the numerical cards stencils were cut and printed in the colours required. Such packs could be produced at a fraction of

the cost of engraved cards, and as a result France soon outstripped Germany as a card-making country. By the sixteenth century it had become the main producer, exporting all over Europe.

French playing-card design was also regional. Until the end of the seventeenth century many new patterns had emerged, but then the law took a hand. Authorities saw a lucrative source of revenue in playing-cards. As it was easier to levy taxes on known patterns, nine regional designs were established in 1701. Those chosen had existed for some time and were the *portraits* or patterns of Lyons, Dauphiné, Provence, Burgundy (also called Lorraine), Auvergne, Limousin (very similar to the Auvergne pattern), Guyenne, Languedoc and Paris. These regional designs were used until 1780, when all regional versions except that of Paris were abolished.

Following the French Revolution, in 1793 the use of all royal emblems on playing-cards was forbidden. The industry was thrown into turmoil, for thousands of wood-blocks would have had to be discarded and new ones made. To meet the new regulations old blocks were hastily refurbished by cutting out the crowns and royalist regalia, which crude designs served until new court

(Right) A representation of courts of the standard Paris pattern as issued during the nineteenth century. (Left) A stencil used to apply colours to the figures on the court cards.

Three cards from a French Revolutionary pack which replaced Kings, Queens and Jacks with Génies, Libertés and Égalités.

14

Above: *The French suits of Diamonds, Hearts, Spades and Clubs.*

Above right: *Two cards from a remarkable Flemish pack dating back to the late fifteenth century. Beautifully preserved and hand-painted in colours, the complete 52-card pack was sold at Sotheby's in 1983 for £90,000. The pack uses suitmarks of Horns, Dog-collars, Double Nooses and Ropes. Shown here are the Jack and Queen of Dog-collars.*

A nineteenth-century pack from France made especially for fortune-telling. Each picture card in the pack has a miniature version of the standard Paris pattern in the corner.

15

Above: *A King of Hearts from a Paris-pattern pack. The crown has been cut away.*
Above right: *A Liberté des Cultes of the Clubs suit and a Génie de la Guerre of the Hearts suit.*
Right: *An attempt to devise a new pattern pack after the French Revolution.*
Below: *Three cards from the Aluette pack which is still found in Brittany. The pack is a version of the Spanish one, and shown here are the Two of Coins, the Knight of Cups and the Ace of Swords. In the Aluette pack the Knights are female.*

cards could be made showing figures without crowns. Kings were replaced by 'Sages', 'Elements' or 'Geniuses'; Queens became 'Virtues', 'Liberties' or 'Seasons'; and Jacks turned into *'Égalités'*, 'Heroes' or 'Cultivators'. These innovations were unpopular, however, and eventually the French pack regained its trappings of royalty. The Paris pattern returned and remains the standard pack in France today.

Although French suitmarks on cards spread throughout France, they did not entirely displace cards with Italian-Spanish suitmarks, for two such packs of cards are still current. One is the Catalan pattern which closely follows the style of Spanish cards, selling, as its name implies, in the Spanish-French border country. The other is found surprisingly in Brittany, where it is used for playing the game of Aluette. The pattern is unique to the area, as is the game.

Many of the ornate patterns produced in places like Rouen were intended for export, and at least two popular patterns emerged. The export business was badly hit by government restrictions, so a number of makers left France to set up business in Holland, Belgium and England. It was the Paris pattern, however, which became popular elsewhere in Europe, particularly in Belgium, Holland and the Scandinavian countries.

PLAYING-CARDS IN ENGLAND AND THE UNITED STATES

Card-playing in England appears to have begun some time in the mid fifteenth century. Our knowledge derives from various written sources, since no early cards have survived. A statute dated 29th September 1464 prohibited playing-cards (referred to as *Cardes a Juer*). A letter dated about 1484, written by Margery Paston to her husband, refers to playing-cards — apparently used on festive occasions. They were certainly familiar to Henry VIII, who tried to suppress them in 1526, and to the Reverend John Northbrooke of Bristol, who in 1576 condemned playing-cards in a sermon as 'an invention of the Devil'.

Nevertheless playing-cards continued to arrive in England, most coming from France but others from Spain, so that Spanish suitmarks were known in England as well as French. Evidence of the early use of Spanish cards in England can be noted from a London advertisement for playing-cards of 1702, which had been 'lately brought from Vigo'. They were 'pleasant to the eye by their curious colours and quite different from ours'. Here the word 'colours' refers to the

The origin of the English pack as shown by the King of Hearts: (left to right) the Rouen pack; an English design of about 1640; an English design of about 1675; and an English card of about 1750.

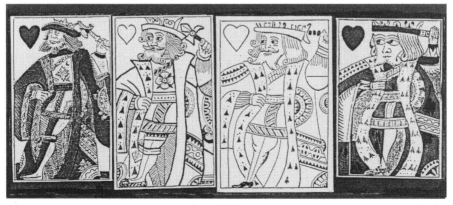

Variations on the English pattern. Top row (left to right): the Queen of Diamonds from a De La Rue pack which appeared about 1880; the Queen of Clubs from a 'Forcolar' pack issued in 1947, in which the suitmarks are coloured red, green, orange and black; the Jack of Hearts from a French version of the English pack issued by A. Camoin and Company. Bottom row: the King of Hearts from a Spanish-made pack which makes the King appear to have three arms; the King of Clubs from a revised version made in Japan; the Jack of Diamonds from a Swedish revision.

Some English cards issued for special occasions and purposes. Top row (left to right): the Queen of Hearts from a satirical 'South Sea Bubble' pack published in 1720; the Ten of Clubs from a 'Marlborough's Victories' pack issued in 1707; the Ace of Diamonds from the 'Knavery of the Rump' pack issued in 1679, which satirised the government of Oliver Cromwell. Bottom row: the Two of Diamonds from a pack showing maps of English and Welsh counties; the Ten of Diamonds from a pack made in 1688 showing arms of English peers; the Queen of Hearts from what is probably the first purpose-made fortune-telling pack made in England — this edition was issued in 1714.

Three modern English-pattern Kings of Diamonds showing variations by different makers. The centre card, by a German maker, has a German-type king at the opposite end.

suitmarks; even today in France and Germany suits are known by this word.

By the time of this advertisement the standard English pattern had become established. With some variations it is the familiar one in use today in Britain and the United States of America. It originated in France and was one of the Rouen patterns referred to in the previous chapter.

The English names for the suits, however, have been influenced by cards from various sources. 'Hearts' is a simple translation of the French *Coeurs,* 'Spades' comes from the Spanish *Espadas* (swords), and 'Clubs' is a translation of Spanish *Bastos.* 'Diamonds' seems to have been a totally English invention, presumably based on the shape of a facet on a cut precious stone.

As in other countries, the authorities were not slow to realise that money could be made by taxing playing-cards. In England this was done by devising a special Ace of Spades, the first of which appeared in 1765. The maker's name was incorporated in this Duty Ace. As no pack could be issued with only three aces, this was a successful way to avoid forgery. These aces had to be obtained from the Stamp Office, the duty being paid at that time. Crude attempts at forgery were made, but offenders were usually caught and sometimes executed.

Printing followed the practice employed in France: wood-blocks were made of the twelve court cards, these being assembled in a printing press and hand-printed in black. When these were dry, the colours were applied by means of several stencils. The numerical cards were usually produced entirely from stencils. Afterwards the sheets were pasted on to suitable board, sometimes with a layer of black in the 'sandwich' to avoid show-through on the final product. The sheets were then cut into individual cards.

The English pack spread throughout the British Isles and was then taken to America by the colonists. Today the United States of America continues to use this pack, although it was not the first pattern to arrive in the New World. It had been preceded by the Spanish pattern, which remains in use in Mexico and the other Latin-American countries.

American card-playing has added one feature to the standard English pack. That is the Joker, now regarded as a standard card in the pack. A feature of the game of euchre, once popular in America, is to call the Jack of the trump suit and the Jack of the suit with the same colour the 'Bower' (from the German *bauer* meaning farmer). There were thus two Bowers in the game until an extra card was introduced and named the 'Best Bower'. Eventually this extra card was renamed the Joker, probably a corrup-tion of the name of the game.

The popularity of games such as whist and bridge has resulted in the English-pattern pack being adopted throughout the world as a standard, particularly in international competitions.

TAROTS AND MINCHIATE CARDS

During the twentieth century, Tarot cards have been the subject of much speculation and discussion. Much has been written on them and their so-called 'mystic powers'. This occult idea largely stems from a six-volumed book by the French author Antoine Court de Gébélin, published in 1781 and entitled *Le Monde Primitif*. This encyclopaedic work states that Tarots are derived from the *Book of Thoth*, a mystical and mythical writing from ancient Egypt. It describes the supposed occult significance of Tarot cards. There is no evidence for Court de Gébélin's statements, but this did not prevent a spate of pseudo-scientific litera-ture appearing.

Tarot cards may appear strange to those people who know only standard playing-cards. If they appear mysterious it is because they are unfamiliar. Tarot cards are simply a variety of playing-cards which are used for a number of card games. They originated in Italy and spread into Austria, southern France and Switzerland. They are found with Latin or French suitmarks, although there are considerable differences between the two types.

The best known and most typical is the Marseilles Tarot. A full pack contains 78 cards, of which 56 are divided into the Italian suits of Coins, Cups, Swords and Batons. Each suit includes four court

The Marseilles Tarot: the King of Cups and trump 16, La Maison Dieu.

cards, King, Queen, Knight and Jack, and ten numerical cards from Ten to Ace. In addition the Tarot pack has 21 special trump cards which bear no suitmarks but which are numbered from 1 to 21. A 22nd card known as the Fool is unnumbered.

Each trump bears a picture, the design of which is thought to have originated during the fifteenth century. The names of these are given on each card; they vary slightly from version to version, but basically are as follows: 1, the Juggler or Mountebank; 2, the Female Pope or High Priestess; 3, the Empress; 4, the Emperor; 5, the Pope; 6, the Lovers or Marriage; 7, the Chariot; 8, Justice; 9, the Hermit or Old Man; 10, the Wheel of Fortune; 11, Fortitude, Strength or Force; 12, the Hanging Man; 13, Death; 14, Temperance; 15, the Devil; 16, the Tower; 17, the Star or Stars; 18, the Moon; 19, the Sun; 20, Judgement; 21, the World. As can be seen, the composition of the Tarot pack is unusual, and it is small wonder that people seeing it for the first time believed it to involve some mysticism.

One of the problems in trying to discover the origin of these cards has been that many packs referred to in older works as 'Tarots' were nothing of the sort.

Tarot packs were once referred to as Triumphs or Trumps, for the name 'Tarot' (in its Italian form *tarocchi)* did not come into use until the beginning of the sixteenth century. The earliest historical reference which can be substantiated comes from the *Registro dei Mandati* for the court of Ferrara, Italy. The year was 1442, and the entry refers to *pare uno de carte da trionfi:* a pack of trump (Tarot) cards. Another reference in the same year in the *Registro de Guardaroba* refers to 'four packs of trump cards'. The lack of earlier evidence seems to indicate an early fifteenth-century origin. There is little doubt that the Tarot pack was an Italian invention which soon became very popular.

No occult values were ever ascribed to Tarot cards until Court de Gébélin wrote his tract. Tarot cards had been known in France for well over two hundred years when Court de Gébélin declared that they were derived from the ancient Egyptian religion. He went so far as to give a derivation of 'Tarot' from the Egyptian *tar* meaning 'way', and, *ro, ros* or *rog* meaning 'royal'. Exactly how he knew

Two cards from a Minchiate pack: trumps 28 (the Goat) and 21 (Water).

Three cards from French-suited Tarot packs: trump 5 from an Austrian pack, the Fool and trump 4 from German packs.

this is unexplained: at the time Champollion had not deciphered the Egyptian hieroglyphics and no one knew what the language was like. The so-called derivation is quite spurious, and the words shown have no meaning at all so far as ancient Egypt is concerned. Notwithstanding his total ignorance of Tarot cards, Egyptian history and language, Court de Gébélin then went on to describe the occultism in each of the Tarot trumps.

Various other occultists and fortune tellers followed Court de Gébélin, saying that the Tarot pack was divided into two parts, the 'Major Arcana' consisting of the 21 trumps and the Fool and the 'Minor Arcana', being the rest of the pack. Some cartomancers — fortune tellers who use cards — use the whole pack for their interpretations, others use only the trumps and the Fool. Whichever method is employed, the cards are dealt in a particular order; but this can vary, even Etteilla, one of Court de Gébélin's disciples, describes a number of methods of laying out the cards. Each card is supposed to have certain characteristics or meanings. Thus trump number 10, the Wheel of Fortune, is said to represent

destiny, worldly luck or success; but if it is inverted it represents bigotry, bias, severity or legal complication. Those who are interested in such things will find many books on the subject.

As to the subjects on the cards themselves, no one knows how they arose. Given that the inventor of the pack needed 21 extra cards to be used as permanent trumps, he would have to approach an artist to produce designs, or call on existing artistic works, books or other printed matter. Undoubtedly many of these would have been series of moralistic designs, probably used as educational aids. It may have been from such sources that the new Tarot pack derived.

The second Tarot type, appearing about a century later, was the Minchiate pack, which was certainly invented in Florence. This newly devised pattern required nineteen new permanent trumps in addition to those used in normal Tarot packs, so the inventor took the twelve signs of the zodiac and added the four elements, Earth, Fire, Air and Water. The Tarot pack already contained Prudence, so he added three more virtues, Faith, Hope and Charity. The result was a new pack of 97 cards.

Italian-suited Tarot packs. Top row (left to right): the Hanging Man (a double-ended card), trump 12 from the Piedmont Tarot; the Queen of Batons from a modern Tarot pack especially designed for the James Bond film 'Live and Let Die'; the Fool from a modern version Tarot made in Spain. Bottom row: the Knight of Money from a Belgian Tarot made in 1770; the Wheel of Fortune, trump 10, from a modernised version of an old Swiss pack; the Lovers, trump 8, from the Sicilian Tarot pack.

Some French-suited Tarots. Top row (left to right): trump 20 from a German Cego (or Tarot) pack; the Knight of Clubs from another German Cego pack; trump 2 from a French Tarot showing country scenes on all trump cards. Bottom row: trump 17 from the Salzburger Tarock, showing scenes from and around the Austrian city; the Knight of Hearts from 'Nuevo Juego del Tarot', a Spanish-made pack showing Alpine figures and scenes on courts and trumps; trump 2 from the standard Austrian Tarot pack, known as 'Industrie und Gluck'.

The Minchiate pack, which survived until the late nineteenth century, was used for a number of card games. It does not appear to have been popular with cartomancers but was almost certainly used by some, who would have devised a yet more complicated system of divination.

Tarot packs with French suitmarks are commonly found in France, Austria, Switzerland and Germany. The full pack contains 78 cards, the designs of which are more modern-looking than those of the Marseilles Tarot. There are the usual four suits of Hearts, Clubs, Diamonds and Spades, each containing fourteen cards including four courts. The main difference lies in the trumps, of which there are 21 plus a Fool. Instead of the archaic designs described, the trumps show scenes which betray the pack's nineteenth-century origin, depicting outdoor pursuits and indoor activities like dances. Some packs, usually found in Germany, have representations of animal life on them. Each trump is double-ended, having a different picture at either end.

Two cards from a French-suited Tarot pack: the Cavalier of Clubs and trump 13.

Three cards from a Japanese 'Hana fuda' pack: September Chrysanthemum ten-point card; July Clover ten-point card; September Chrysanthemum one-point card.

ORIENTAL PLAYING-CARDS

Although European cards are widely used in all countries of the East, there remain five countries where local playing-cards still exist.

JAPAN

As well as producing a large quantity of western cards — mainly for export — the most popular indigenous playing-cards are called *Hana* cards, or *Hana fuda*. Such packs consist of 48 cards and like almost all local ones are quite small. They measure about 54 by 33 mm (2⅛ by 1¼ inches), are printed on one side only and are quite thick (about 1 mm, just under ¹⁄₁₆ inch). A complete set of *Hana* cards consists of two packs, distinguished by variant colours on the back, such as one black and one red.

The designs are very attractive, each card being a different flower design. A *Hana* pack is divided into twelve suits, one for each month. Certain cards in each suit have additional features, perhaps birds, animals or other subjects such as bridges, curtains or wine cups. These alter the playing value of the card concerned. Although now printed on card, *Hana fuda* may be found hand-painted on

small flat seashells.

Hana are by far the most popular Japanese cards, but there are other varieties used in 'matching' games such as the Hundred Poets, which contains one hundred pairs of cards in each pack, each card depicting a Japanese poet or scene. Another large pack contains over four hundred cards showing short classical poems. One 96-card game is based on the Japanese alphabet: half the cards show pictures, the rest text.

The last group of Japanese cards is very important, and although considered to be typically Japanese they are derived from European cards. The Portuguese arrived in Japan in 1543 bringing their own cards with them. These cards were accepted by the Japanese but over the centuries have become so stylised that their origin is difficult to discern. However, they are of certain Portuguese origin, retaining the suitmarks of Cups, Swords, Coins and Batons *(Koppu, Isu, Oru* and *Ho)*. Such packs have ten or so variants, some omitting certain suits, others repeating cards. All are printed in a manner and size similar to *Hana* cards, although the designs are quite different.

27

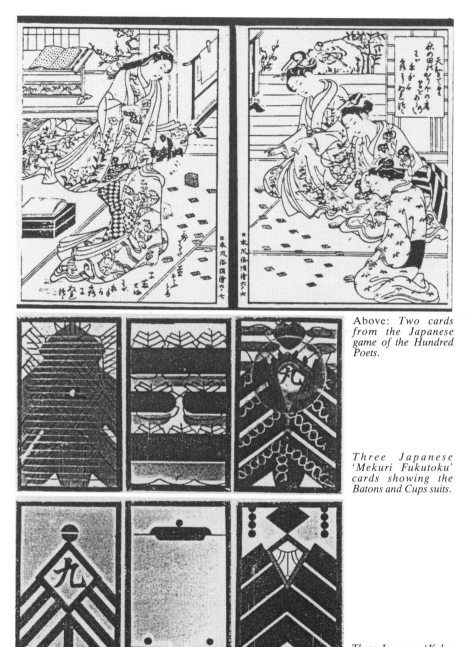

Above: *Two cards from the Japanese game of the Hundred Poets.*

Three Japanese 'Mekuri Fukutoku' cards showing the Batons and Cups suits.

Three Japanese 'Kabu Kinseizan' cards with suits of Batons and Cups.

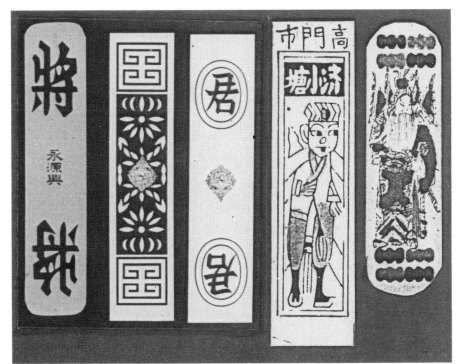

Chinese-type chess, money and domino playing-cards.

CHINA

Cards are said to have existed at least as early as the T'ang Dynasty (AD 618 to 907), but this remains to be proved. Until recently all playing-cards were regarded with some disfavour in the People's Republic, undoubtedly because the Chinese are great gamblers, and their playing-cards are used almost entirely to this end.

These cards are always long and narrow, although the actual packs vary somewhat in size from about 65 by 20 mm (2½ by ¾ inches) to 120 by 30 mm (4¾ by 1⅛ inches). They fall into six principal groups: mah-jong, word or phrase cards, number cards, money cards, domino or dice cards, and chess cards.

Although mah-jong is usually made as sets of tiles it is in effect a card game by character, and one can buy packs of mah-jong cards. The game is based on an elaborate version of the three-suited money pack (see below). It contains 136 cards or tiles consisting of three suits of nine cards repeated four times. In addition there are four winds and three dragons, also repeated four times. Mah-jong suits consist of Bamboos, Circles and Characters, each numbered from one to nine in either Chinese or European numerals. Some packs have one or two sets of flower cards in addition, named Spring, Summer, Autumn and Winter, and the Fisher, the Woodcutter, the Farmer and the Scholar.

Word and phrase cards are very Chinese in appearance, and indeed impossible to comprehend without a knowledge of the Chinese language.

Money packs consist of thirty or forty cards repeated three or four times. There are three or four suits, and even 'court' cards, so there is some basic similarity to western cards. Chinese suitmarks are related to coins called *cash*. It has been said that the original playing-cards were paper banknotes, printed at a time of gross inflation, and used as instruments

29

of gambling.

The suits consist of various groups of coins: single coins, strings of coins, myriads of coins, or variations of these.

Domino cards are like ordinary western dominoes, but the spots are in two colours in various combinations, usually black and red. There are 21 basic cards with different spot combinations, and packs repeat these four to six times.

Chess cards are based on Chinese chess, which can be either four- or two-sided. To western eyes they have rather a dull and plain appearance, but they are of considerable interest to researchers for it is said that European cards may have been derived from four-sided chess.

A Chinese chess pack has 28 basic cards divided into four suits, which are indicated simply by the colour of the card. (Compare the European languages which refer to suits as 'colours'.) Each suit contains seven cards representing the chess pieces, but not all suits have the same pieces. Green and White suits each contain a General, an Official, an Elephant, a Cannon, a Horse, a Cart and a Soldier. Red and Yellow suits have a General, an Official, a Minister, a Cannon, a Horse, a Battle Wagon and a Soldier. As with other Chinese packs, these 28 cards are repeated a number of times. Obviously, the constituent parts of the Chinese chess pack are quite different from any pack of European cards.

KOREA

The playing-cards produced in Korea bear a resemblance to those of China. The cards are very long and narrow, however, measuring about 160 by 15 mm (6¼ by ⅝ inches). They are simple in design, being inscribed in black on orange, usually on one side only. A full pack contains eighty cards in eight suits, representing Men, Fish, Crows, Pheasants, Antelopes, Stars, Rabbits and Horses. None of these is illustrated on the cards, identification being by captions only. Sometimes the reverse side is printed with a symbol denoting an arrowhead or feather.

INDIA

Playing-cards in India are called *ganjifa* and almost all are circular. They vary in size from small discs about 25 mm (1 inch) across, to much larger ones over 100 mm (4 inches) in diameter. They are always made by hand using any material — paper, thin wood, ivory, leather, fish-scales or leaves. They are painted

Two cards from the Persian or Iranian game of As Nas showing the 'Shah' (King) and 'Bibi' (Queen).

Two court cards from an Indian 'ganjifa' pack. ·

and lacquered several times, producing a final disc of some bulk.

The earliest known reference to Indian playing-cards is found in the writings of Baber, the first Mogul emperor, who sent a pack of *ganjifa* to Sind in the year 1527. A later reference by Akbar the Great gives a date of 1590, but there is little doubt that Indian playing-cards were well known by this date. A few early packs show an obvious Portuguese influence.

Ganjifa packs are suited, although the number of suits can vary from four to eighteen or even more: some packs contain as many as 360 cards. Exactly how games were played with such an unwieldy number is hard to say. Packs use religious, military or astrological ideas, the court cards being deities, divinities, war-riors and others, and the many suitmarks including animals, umbrellas, bows and arrows, vases, shells, and so on.

Since all the cards are made by hand, the workmanship varies considerably from very crude to exquisite.

IRAN

Ganjifa packs similar to those used in India are also known in Iran, although there is also a local Iranian pack called *As Nas*. Like Indian packs it is hand-made but is rectangular in shape. There are 25 cards in a pack, consisting of cards representing the Shah, the Queen, the Dancing Girl, the Lion (or Eagle or Dragon) and the Soldier. These are repeated five times.

FURTHER READING

Beal, George. *Playing-cards and Their Story*. David and Charles, 1975.
Benham, W. Gurney. *Playing-cards*. Ward Lock, 1931.
Denning, Trevor. *Spanish Playing-cards*. IPCS, 1980.
Dummett, Michael. *The Game of Tarot*. Duckworth, 1980.
Hargrave, Catherine Perry. *A History of Playing-cards*. Dover, New York, 1966.
Hoffmann, Detlef. *The Playing-card*. Edition Leipzig, 1973.
Huson, Paul. *The Devil's Picturebook*. Abacus, 1972.
Mann, Sylvia. *Collecting English Playing-cards*. Stanley Gibbons, 1978.
Mann, Sylvia. *Collecting Playing Cards*. Howard Baker, 1979.
Morley, H. T. *Old and Curious Playing Cards*. London, 1931.
Tilley, Roger. *Playing Cards*. Weidenfeld and Nicolson, 1967.
Tilley, Roger. *A History of Playing Cards*. Studio Vista, 1973.
Whiting, J. R. S. *A Handful of History*. Alan Sutton, Dursley, 1978.

PLACES TO VISIT

GREAT BRITAIN
Bodleian Library, Oxford OX1 3BG. Telephone: Oxford (0865) 277000.
British Museum, Great Russell Street, London WC1B 3DG. Telephone: 01-636 1555.
Guildhall Library, Aldermanbury, London EC2P 2EJ. Telephone: 01-606 3030.
Victoria and Albert Museum, Cromwell Road, South Kensington, London SW7 2RL. Telephone: 01-938 8500.

AUSTRIA
Albertina Collection of Graphic Arts, Augustinerstrasse 1, 1010 Vienna.
Stadtmuseum Linz, Bethlehemstrasse 7, 4020 Linz, Oberösterreich.

BELGIUM
Nationaal Museum van der Speelkaart, Begijnenstraat 26, 2300 Turnhout, Antwerp.

EAST GERMANY
Spielkartenmuseum, Schloss Altenburg, 7400 Altenburg.

FRANCE
Bibliothèque de l'Arsenal, Rue de Sully, Paris.
Bibliothèque Municipale, Rue Jacques Villon, Rouen, Seine-Maritime.
Bibliothèque Nationale, Rue de Richelieu, 75084 Paris.

NETHERLANDS
Amsterdams Historisches Museum, Nieuwzijds Voorburgwal 359, Kalverstraat 92, 1012 PH Amsterdam.

SPAIN
Museu de Naipes, Calle Heraclio Fournier, Vitoria, Alava.

SWITZERLAND
Historisches Museum Basel, Barfüsserkirche, 4052 Basel.

UNITED STATES OF AMERICA
Beinecke Library, Yale University, 203 New Haven, Connecticut 06510.
Cincinnati Art Museum, Eden Park, Cincinnati, Ohio 45202.
Metropolitan Museum of Art, 5th Avenue at 82nd Street, New York, NY 10028.
Pierpont Morgan Library, 29 East 36th Street, New York, NY 10016.
Players Card Museum, 4 Main Avenue, Newley, Pennsylvania 18428.

WEST GERMANY
Deutsches Spielkarten-Museum, Schönbuchstrasse 32, 7022 Leinfelden Echterdingen, Baden-Württemberg.
Germanisches National-Museum, Kornmarkt 1, 8500 Nuremberg, Bavaria.
Historisches Museum Frankfurt, Saalgasse 19, 6000 Frankfurt 1, Hessen.

Those interested in the collection or historical study of playing-cards are recommended to join the International Playing-card Society (IPCS), 188 Sheen Lane, East Sheen, London SW14 8LF. Two quarterly publications are issued: *The Playing-card* and *Playing-card World.*